Ripley's Believe It or Not!

Developed and produced by Ripley Publishing Ltd

This edition published and distributed by:

Mason Crest
450 Parkway Drive, Suite D, Broomall, PA 19008
www.masoncrest.com

Printed and bound in the United States of America

First printing
9 8 7 6 5 4 3 2 1

Ripley's Believe It or Not!
Extreme Endeavors
ISBN: 978-1-4222-2780-0 (hardback)
ISBN: 978-1-4222-2797-8 (paperback)
ISBN: 978-1-4222-9041-5 (e-book)
Ripley's Believe It or Not!—Complete 8 Title Series
ISBN: 978-1-4222-2769-5

Cataloging-in-Publication Data on file with the Library of Congress

PUBLISHER'S NOTE
While every effort has been made to verify the accuracy of the entries in this book, the
Publisher's cannot be held responsible for any errors contained in the work. They would
be glad to receive any information from readers.

WARNING
Some of the stunts and activities in this book are undertaken by experts and should not
be attempted by anyone without adequate training and supervision.

Ripley's Believe It or Not!

Enter If You Dare

EXTREME ENDEAVORS

www.MasonCrest.com

Ripley's
Believe It or No
GATLINBURG, TENNESS
www.ripleysbelieveitornot.co

EXTREME ENDEAVORS

Phenomenal feats. Look inside and find superhuman skills and fearless daredevils. Read about the death-defying Spanish bull-leapers, the stunt diver who "bellyflops" from over 35 ft (10.6 m) into 12 in (30 cm) of water, and the very messy World Gravy Wrestling Championships.

Sword swallowers from around the world performed at Ripley Odditoriums for International Sword Swallowers Day...

Both Mike and his yacht were fitted with the latest hi-tech equipment to survive the harsh conditions.

When Mike and his boat were in South Africa for repairs, he met 75-year-old Japanese sailor Minoru Saito, who was in the middle of his eighth circumnavigation of the globe. During his lifetime, Minoru has sailed almost 310,685 mi (500,000 km), the equivalent of sailing to the Moon.

At home in his cabin—containing bunk, galley, supplies, and navigation equipment—Mike catches up on studying for his driving test.

Mike lets off flares to celebrate his return to England after nine months at sea.

AGED JUST 17, MIKE PERHAM FROM HERTFORDSHIRE, ENGLAND, COMPLETED A SINGLE-HANDED, ROUND-THE-WORLD SAILING VOYAGE IN AUGUST 2009. THE INTREPID TEENAGER SET OFF FROM PORTSMOUTH, ENGLAND, IN NOVEMBER 2008—THEN AGED ONLY 16—ON BOARD A HI-TECH 50-FT (15-M) RACING YACHT HIRED ESPECIALLY FOR THE CHALLENGE. THE CIRCUMNAVIGATION TOOK MIKE DOWN THE WEST COAST OF AFRICA AND SOUTH OF AUSTRALIA, WHERE DAMAGE TO THE YACHT'S RUDDER FORCED HIM TO WAIT FOR REPAIRS BEFORE SETTING OFF INTO THE TREACHEROUS SOUTHERN OCEAN. HERE, THE BOAT BATTLED THROUGH FREEZING SEAS AND 50-FT (15-M) SWELLS. FIFTY-KNOT (57-MPH) WINDS KNOCKED THE BOAT FLAT TO THE WAVES BEFORE THE HEAVY KEEL PULLED IT UPRIGHT. MIKE WAS FORCED TO CLIMB THE 70-FT (21-M) MAST IN THE MIDDLE OF THE OCEAN TO FIX RIGGING IN THE KNOCKDOWN, AND HAD TO DIVE UNDER THE BOAT TO CUT FREE SNAGGED ROPES. THE YACHT THEN SAILED UP THE COAST OF SOUTH AMERICA AND THROUGH THE PANAMA CANAL BEFORE THE FINAL LEG OF THE JOURNEY TOOK MIKE ACROSS THE ATLANTIC, LANDING AT PORTSMOUTH IN AUGUST: NINE MONTHS AND 24,233 MI (39,000 KM) LATER. THE LIGHT, HI-SPEED RACING YACHT WAS CRAMPED, NOISY, AND UNCOMFORTABLE, MAKING IT VERY HARD TO GET REST. MIKE SLEPT FOR ABOUT FIVE HOURS OUT OF EVERY 24, SNATCHING 20-MINUTE NAPS WHILE THE BOAT WAS KEPT ON COURSE BY AN ELECTRONIC AUTOPILOT. WITH NOBODY ELSE ON DECK, THERE WAS A DANGER OF COLLIDING WITH VESSELS AT NIGHT AND RAMMING SURFACE HAZARDS SUCH AS SHIPPING CONTAINERS AND MARINE DEBRIS. MIKE WAS HARNESSED TO THE BOAT AT ALL TIMES IN CASE HE WAS SWEPT OVERBOARD AND ALL OF HIS FOOD WAS FREEZE-DRIED AND RATIONED.

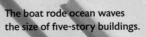

The boat rode ocean waves the size of five-story buildings.

WORLD BEATER

Mike had to climb the 70-ft (21-m) mast in the middle of the ocean to carry out repairs.

ⓇIPLEY'S ask

What drove you to start this challenge?
At 14 I became the youngest person to sail solo across the Atlantic. Once I had done that, I knew the next step was to sail around the world alone.

Was the hi-tech boat uncomfortable? How did you sleep?
Totallymoney.com is an Open 50 racing yacht. She is fast, functional, and like a racing car...very basic inside. I had a transverse bunk running across the front of the navigation station and the galley consisted of a small sink and single-burner stove. I had to be alert the whole time, even when asleep! I got into the routine of cat-napping for 20 minutes at a time, then checking the boat and adjusting the sails or course. If the motion suddenly changed, my subconscious sensed it immediately and I would wake

up. I also had alarms on the radar, depth sounder, and chart plotter that would warn me of anything untoward, though none of these things could identify an iceberg.

What was the toughest part of the trip?
Being away from friends and family. Also, I had to climb the mast three times to make repairs and I don't like heights.

Were you ever worried?
Certainly.

What was the most memorable part of the voyage?
The Southern Ocean without doubt. It was cold and wet down there, but it was certainly exciting. I was surfing along at speeds very close to 30 knots (35 mph) and they were by far the best experiences. I was wearing a grin from ear to ear during those days.

Were you glad to get back on dry land?
It was fantastic to get back and fulfill my dream of becoming the youngest person to sail solo around the world. To get such a big reception and see all my friends and family on the dock was just the icing on the cake. It took a few days to get into the routine of sleeping through the night, but I settled in surprisingly easy and it was fantastic to be back with all my friends.

Do you have any future sailing plans?
The next plan is the *Bounty* boat expedition. In a nutshell, four of us are going to re-enact Capt. William Bligh's 4,000-mi (6,450-km) voyage across the Pacific in an open boat following the story of the *Mutiny on the Bounty*, sailing from Tonga across to Timor!

Walking in the Air

In August 2009, aged just eight years old, Tiger Brewer from London, England, stood on the top of a biplane flown by his grandfather at 100 mph (160 km/h). His wing-walking feat took place at a height of 1,000 ft (304 m) above Rendcomb airfield in Gloucestershire, England, and followed a family tradition—Tiger's grandfather, Vic Norman, manages SuperAeroBatics, the world's only formation wing-walking team.

ℛ BEGINNER'S LUCK

In March 2009, a 62-year-old Norwegian, Unni Haskell, hit a hole-in-one with her first ever swing on a golf course. Mrs. Haskell had received just two months of lessons before taking aim on the 100-yd (91-m) hole in St. Petersburg, Florida.

ℛ YOUNG HUSTLER

Keith O'Dell Jr. of Gloversville, New York State, plays pool for up to three hours a day—even though he is just two years old.

ℛ BLIND BOXER

Bashir Ramathan of Kampala, Uganda, has been blind for over a decade but has recently resumed his career as a professional boxer.

Trunk Ball ⬇

THE UNUSUAL SPORT OF ELEPHANT POLO WAS FIRST PLAYED IN INDIA IN THE EARLY 20TH CENTURY, BUT THE MODERN GAME ORIGINATED IN NEPAL IN 1983 WHERE THE GAME IS NOW A REGISTERED OLYMPIC SPORT. TOURNAMENTS, PLAYED IN THAILAND, NEPAL, AND SRI LANKA, DRAW IN 12 INTERNATIONAL TEAMS EVERY YEAR FROM FIVE DIFFERENT CONTINENTS AND ARE ORGANIZED BY THE WEPA (WORLD ELEPHANT POLO ASSOCIATION). EACH MATCH INVOLVES 28 ELEPHANTS, EACH WITH TWO PLAYERS ON ITS BACK, AND MAHOUTS (DRIVERS) CONTROLLING THE ELEPHANTS. THE GAME IS PLAYED ON AN AREA THE SIZE OF A FOOTBALL FIELD AND PLAYERS WIELD POLO STICKS THAT ARE 6–9 FT (1.8–2.7 M) IN LENGTH.

Elephant Polo RULES

- ○ Elephants must not lie down in front of the goalmouth
- ○ An elephant may not pick up a ball with its trunk during play
- ○ Elephants must not step on the ball
- ○ No team may have more than three elephants on one half of the field at any given time
- ○ Sex, age, or size of the elephant does not matter
- ○ Men may use only one hand to hold onto the elephant, women may use two

It's All Gravy

The World Gravy Wrestling Championships took place in Lancashire, England, in 2009, to raise money for charity. A leading gravy-powder manufacturer provided 440 gallons (2,000 l) of gravy for the contest—the equivalent of 40,000 portions—for the 16 competitors to battle in. The overall winner was "Stone Cold Steve Bisto," aka Joel Hicks, a 30-year-old barrister who was watched by hundreds as he took the crown after having competed for three years in a row.

® VOLCANO BOARDING

In the new sport of volcano boarding, thrill-seekers race at speeds of up to 50 mph (80 km/h) down the sides of an active volcano. Dressed in protective jumpsuits, kneepads, and helmets, competitors hurtle down Nicaragua's 2,382-ft-high (726-m) Cerro Negro mountain—which has erupted 20 times since 1850, the last as recently as 1999—on specially constructed plywood boards.

® VETERAN BOWLER

Emma Hendrickson from Morris Plains, New Jersey, took part in the United States' Ten-Pin Bowling Championships in April 2009—at 100 years of age!

® WATER JUMP

In July 2009, 13-year-old Charlotte Wharton from Northamptonshire, England, leaped a distance of nearly 100 ft (30.5 m) on water skis. Charlotte, who had been skiing for just two years, soared nearly 50 ft (15 m) high in the air at 30 mph (48 km/h) as she jumped 98 ft 8 in (30.1 m), which is the equivalent of three school buses parked end to end.

® PLUCKY PITCHER

Bert Shepard pitched for the Washington Senators Major League baseball team despite having lost a leg as a fighter pilot during World War II.

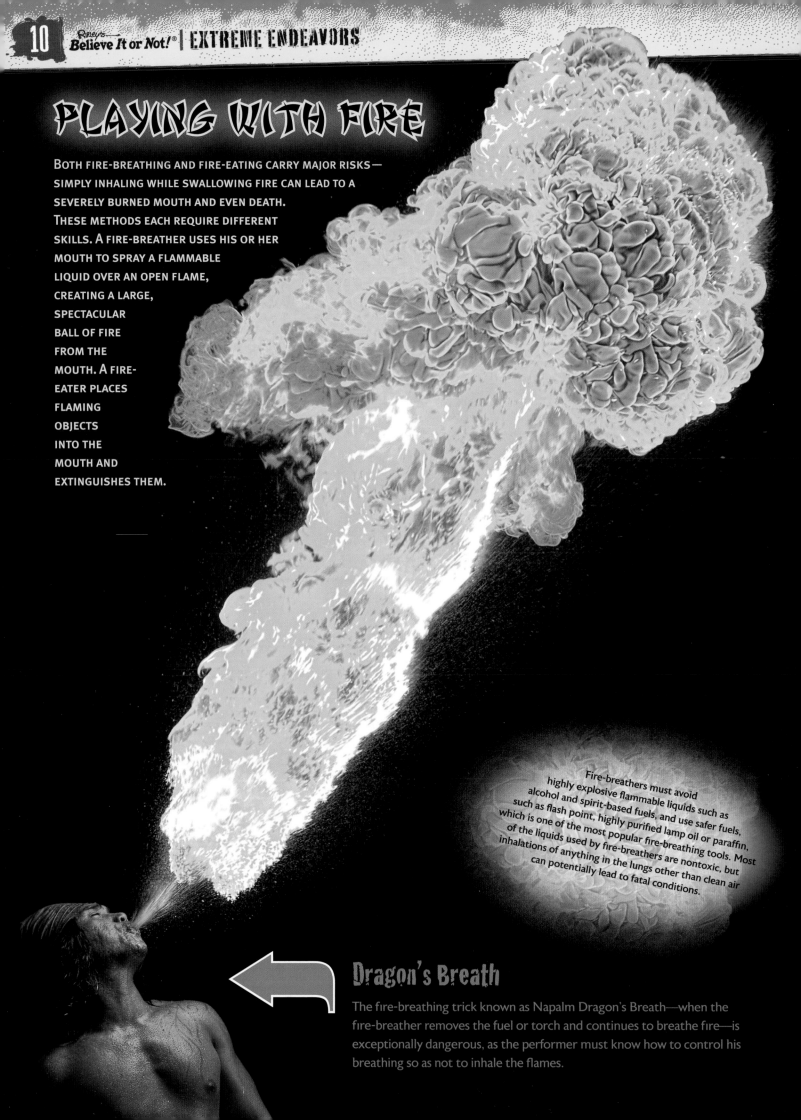

PLAYING WITH FIRE

BOTH FIRE-BREATHING AND FIRE-EATING CARRY MAJOR RISKS—SIMPLY INHALING WHILE SWALLOWING FIRE CAN LEAD TO A SEVERELY BURNED MOUTH AND EVEN DEATH. THESE METHODS EACH REQUIRE DIFFERENT SKILLS. A FIRE-BREATHER USES HIS OR HER MOUTH TO SPRAY A FLAMMABLE LIQUID OVER AN OPEN FLAME, CREATING A LARGE, SPECTACULAR BALL OF FIRE FROM THE MOUTH. A FIRE-EATER PLACES FLAMING OBJECTS INTO THE MOUTH AND EXTINGUISHES THEM.

Fire-breathers must avoid highly explosive flammable liquids such as alcohol and spirit-based fuels, and use safer fuels, such as flash point, highly purified lamp oil or paraffin, which is one of the most popular fire-breathing tools. Most of the liquids used by fire-breathers are nontoxic, but inhalations of anything in the lungs other than clean air can potentially lead to fatal conditions.

Dragon's Breath

The fire-breathing trick known as Napalm Dragon's Breath—when the fire-breather removes the fuel or torch and continues to breathe fire—is exceptionally dangerous, as the performer must know how to control his breathing so as not to inhale the flames.

RIPLEY'S RESEARCH

FIRE-EATERS: TAKE A DEEP BREATH AND BEGIN TO EXHALE SLOWLY AS THE LIGHTED TORCH IS LOWERED TOWARD THE MOUTH. THIS KEEPS THE HEAT AWAY FROM THE PERFORMER'S FACE. WITH THE TONGUE WIDE AND FLAT, THE FIRE-EATER PLACES THE WICK OF THE TORCH (WHICH SHOULD BE COOL TO THE TOUCH) ONTO THE TONGUE AND PARTIALLY CLOSES THE LIPS AROUND THE TORCH IN AN "O" SHAPE. TO EXTINGUISH THE FLAME, THE LIPS CAN EITHER BE CLOSED ENTIRELY AROUND THE TORCH, THUS CUTTING OFF THE OXYGEN SUPPLY, OR THE FLAME CAN BE PUT OUT BY MEANS OF A QUICK EXHALING BREATH.

FIRE-BREATHERS: AVOID HIGHLY EXPLOSIVE FLAMMABLE LIQUIDS, SUCH AS ALCOHOL, AND USE SAFER FUELS SUCH AS PARAFFIN. FIRE-BREATHERS ALWAYS CHECK THE WIND DIRECTION BEFORE THEY PERFORM AND CARRY A CLOTH TO WIPE FUEL FROM THE MOUTH IN BETWEEN BREATHING, SO AS NOT TO SET THEMSELVES ON FIRE. BREATHERS WITH BEARDS TAKE EXTRA CARE WHEN WIPING AWAY THE FLAMMABLE SUBSTANCE!

THERE ARE NO REAL TRICKS TO WORKING WITH FIRE. PERFORMERS HAVE TO REMEMBER THAT HEAT TRAVELS UPWARD AND THEY MUST BE PREPARED TO ENDURE PAIN. TOLERATING BLISTERS ON THE TONGUE, THROAT, AND LIPS IS ALL PART OF THE JOB.

HISTORY HOT SPOT

Robert Powell was the most famous of the early fire-eaters. He performed in London in the 18th century, charging a shilling for entry to his shows, at which he would eat hot coals and melted sealing wax, and lick a naked flame with his tongue. He also used to take a large bunch of matches, light them, and hold them in his mouth until the flame was extinguished, and he sometimes filled his mouth with red-hot charcoal.

A Close Shave

In the late-1930s American Dr. Mayfield, a popular fire manipulator, came to the forefront of the fire-performing world when he appeared at Ripley's Odditoriums. His act involved shaving himself with a "blazing blowtorch" before putting the torch into his mouth and extinguishing it.

Fire-ing Solo

The following fire-breathing stunts have been developed over the centuries and are known as "One Person Blasts."

45-degree Fire Blast 45-degree up angle, one of the most basic fire-breathing tricks

Camp Fire Flame is directly bounced off the ground

Hell Fire Fireball is breathed straight down and the performer rises as the flames engulf him

Carousel Whilst rotating through a full circle, the performer creates a long horizontal blast

Corkscrew Almost vertical duration blast while the breather spins under it

Popcorn Breather performs three or more short blasts of fire without refueling

Serpent Performer breathes alternative up and down horizontal flames while walking

Moving Fire Breather lights a torch held 3 ft (1 m) from the ignition torch with a sustained blast

R CADDIE TREK

In July 2009, Billy Foster, the caddie for English golfer Lee Westwood, walked the 88 mi (142 km) from the Scottish Open tournament at Loch Lomond to the following week's British Open at Turnberry.

R CHESS MASTER

In February 2009, over a period of 14 hours, Bulgarian grandmaster Kiril Georgiev played 360 games of chess simultaneously. He won 284 games, drew 70, and lost only six.

Giant Leap for Mankind

Who was the first man in space? Believe it or not, it was not an astronaut, it was test pilot Joe Kittinger. In 1960, he was assigned to discover whether an astronaut could survive an aborted mission, even 20 mi (32 km) above the Earth. Kittinger rose to 102,800 ft (31,330 m) by balloon, and then jumped out. He was so high that initially he felt no wind resistance. He fell for 4 minutes 36 seconds, reaching a maximum speed of 614 mph (988 km/h), before opening his parachute at 18,000 ft (5,500 m).

R BALL JUGGLER

Dan Magness from Milton Keynes, Buckinghamshire, England, used his feet, legs, and head to keep a soccer ball in the air for 24 hours in May 2009.

R SOLO TEAM

Bob Holmes of Rumney, New Hampshire, has played almost 17,000 volleyball games as a one-man team—and has beaten police departments, professional sports teams, and a team consisting of more than 1,000 people. He has faced over 400,000 opposing players in that time, but has suffered fewer than 400 defeats.

R COLOSSAL PUTT

Irish TV and radio presenter Terry Wogan holed an incredible 99-ft (30-m) putt at Gleneagles golf course in Scotland during a BBC pro–celebrity match in 1981.

R BRAVE SURFER

Aged 18, Bethany Hamilton finished runner-up in the World Junior Women's Surfing Championships in January 2009—despite having lost an arm to a shark five years previously. Bethany was surfing near her home in Hawaii in October 2003 when she was mauled by a 15-ft-long (4.5-m) tiger shark, but within just three weeks she was back on her board.

R ONE-ARMED PLAYER

Despite being born without a right hand and forearm, Poland's Natalia Partyka competes in table tennis competitions for able-bodied athletes and even represented her country at the 2008 Beijing Olympics.

R TENNIS ACE

Over a period of five years, Swiss tennis player Roger Federer reached at least the semifinals of more than 20 consecutive Grand Slam tournaments, and from 2005 to 2007 he reached ten consecutive Grand Slam finals. Between his first-round loss at Wimbledon in 2002 and his defeat in the 2008 Wimbledon final, he won 65 matches in a row on grass.

Sink or Swim

Amsterdam-based designer Diddo believes wetsuits shouldn't be limited to boring black, and a shark-attack pattern is just one of his designs—for surfers who wish to leave the water looking as if they have been attacked by sharks. His other designs include a muscle model, a whale-shark pattern, and a rusted-iron look, evoking the metal diving suits of old.

MAN Vs BEAST

Spanish bull-leapers in Valencia (known as "recortadores") carry on a tradition that goes back to 1500 BC. They face a bull as it charges and, at precisely the right moment, jump over the speeding horns — toes pointed, arms aloft. Spectators watch as the competitors somersault, twirl, and twist through the air, for up to four hours at a time, at every moment risking death or serious injury. The bull always remains unharmed.

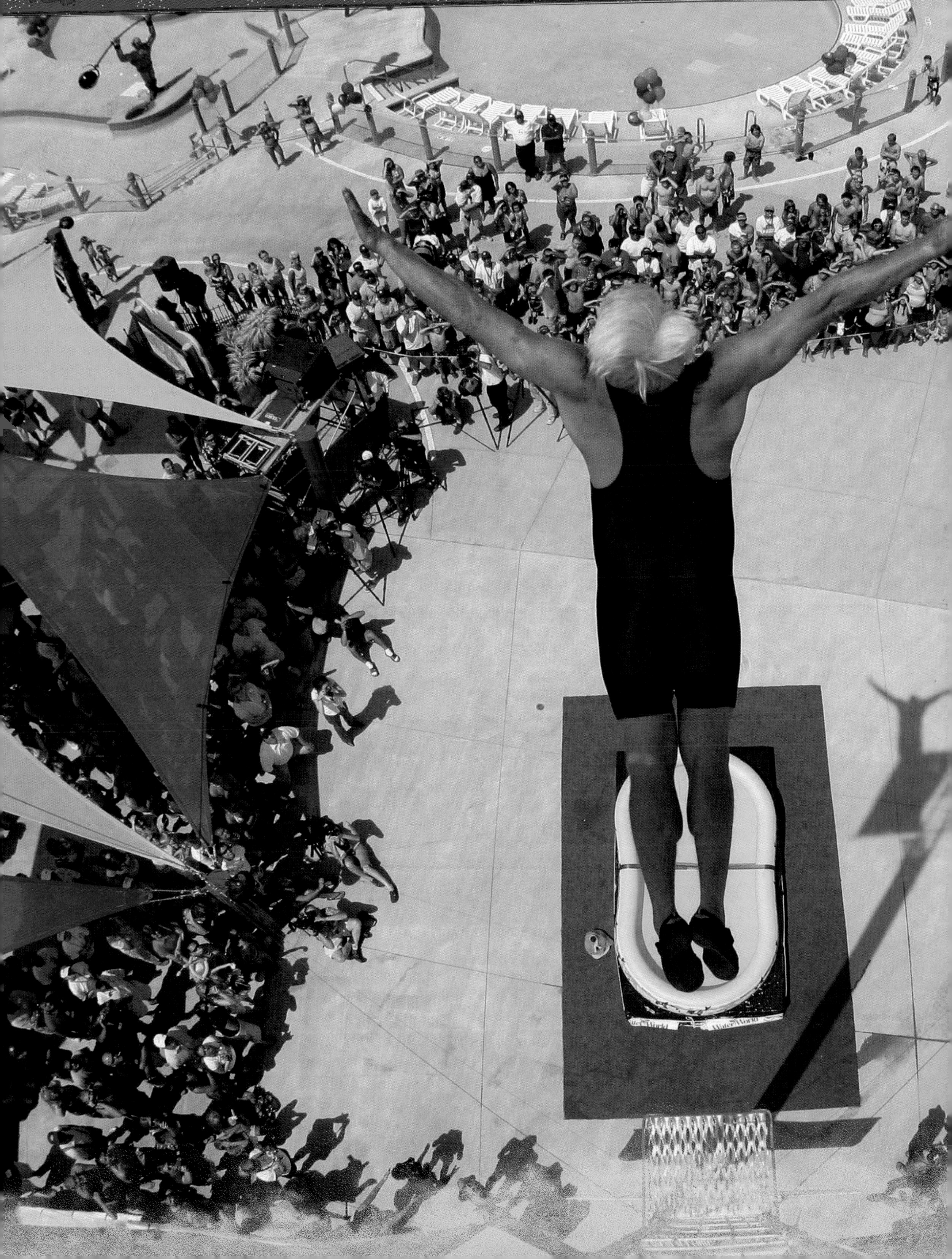

Splash Landing

After his incredible shallow-water plunges were featured in *Ripley's Believe It or Not! Prepare to be Shocked*, daredevil diver Darren Taylor, also known as Professor Splash, from Colorado has now dropped into just 12 in (30 cm) of water from an even greater height of 35 ft 9 in (10.9 m), emerging soaked, but unharmed. Although his "bellyflop" technique might look painful, by stretching as he falls, Professor Splash reduces the impact on his body when he hits the water.

DART WALL

German 13-year-old Maiko Kiesewetter scaled a wall of regular-sized playing darts 16 ft (5 m) high in his hometown of Hamburg in November 2009.

℞ SHADOWBOXERS

To celebrate the first anniversary of the Beijing Olympic Games, nearly 34,000 people gathered in the Chinese capital city in August 2009 and simultaneously performed *taiji*, the martial art of shadowboxing.

℞ GREAT CATCH

Fishing on Lake Minnetonka, Minnesota, in 2008, Jeff Kolodzinski caught 1,680 fish in 24 hours.

℞ HAVING A BALL

Rikki Cunningham played billiards nonstop for 72 hours in Greensboro, North Carolina, in August 2009. During that time, he played 80 different opponents.

℞ HIGH TEE

A team from Bay College, Michigan, created a wooden golf tee that was over 26½ft (8 m) tall—80 times bigger than a normal tee. The head measured 35 in (90 cm) in diameter and the whole tee weighed almost a ton.

Keel Walk

English sailor Alex Thomson decided that he wanted to see the sea from a different angle, so he clambered out onto the keel of his 60-ft (18-m) racing yacht when it was fully keeled over and sailing hard off the south coast of England. The experienced ocean racer, who braved the waves in a smart suit provided by his sponsor, said that it was "pretty dangerous but a real buzz."

℞ BASKETBALL BEGINNER

Despite never having played basketball before, S. Ramesh Babu of Bangalore, India, scored 243 baskets in an hour—that's an average of just over four baskets a minute.

℞ MAGIC MINK

In 2008, 73-year-old Ken Mink made the basketball team at Roane State Community College in Harriman, Tennessee—52 years after his last college game. The veteran even made two free throws as King College's B team were beaten 93–42.

℞ POLE RACE

Rune Malterud and Stian Aker of Norway skied nearly continuously for 17 days 11 hours to win the Amundsen South Pole Race, crossing Antarctica to reach the South Pole before five other teams.

℞ BALL JUGGLER

In May 2009, at San Marcos, California, Abraham Muñoz of the United States ran 3,280 ft (1,000 m) in under five minutes while keeping a soccer ball continuously airborne with his feet.

ℝ SEVEN MARATHONS

Richard Donovan from Galway, Ireland, completed seven marathons on seven continents in less than six days. He began his challenge in sub-zero temperatures in Antarctica on January 31, 2009, and after running marathons in South Africa, Dubai, England, Canada, and Chile, crossed the finish line in Sydney, Australia, just five days, ten hours and eight minutes later. He ran a total of 183 mi (295 km) in 130 hours, enduring extreme temperatures and sleeping only in the economy-class seats of airplanes on his flights between continents.

ℝ EVEREST MATCH

Two teams of English cricketers trekked nine days to the slopes of Mount Everest in April 2009 to a play a game of cricket at an altitude of 16,945 ft (5,165 m). The challenge was the idea of cricket enthusiast Richard Kirtley who had noticed that Everest's Gorak Shep, the highest plateau of its size in the world, resembled London's famous Oval cricket ground.

ℝ BASEBALL BASH

Mike Filippone of North Babylon, New York, swung at nearly 7,000 baseball pitches over a period of 13½ hours in August 2009.

ℝ LONG DRIVE

A golf course stretching along 848 mi (1,365 km) of desert highway opened in Australia in 2009. The Nullarbor Links spans two time zones, measures more than the entire length of Britain, and has holes at 18 towns and service stations. After finishing a hole, golfers have to drive up to 62 mi (100 km) to the next tee and it takes up to four days to complete a round.

ℝ 36-HOUR GAME

In April 2009, at Bristol, England, two soccer teams played a charity match that lasted 36 hours and produced more than 500 goals.

WILD ROLLER

EXTREME INLINE SKATER DIRK AUER FROM GERMANY REACHED INCREDIBLE SPEEDS OF MORE THAN 180 MPH (290 KM/H) WHILE BEING DRAGGED BEHIND A HIGH-POWERED MOTORBIKE AT A RACETRACK IN GERMANY. DIRK HAS ALSO SKATED ON THE ROOF OF AN AIRBORNE PLANE AND DOWN A ROLLER COASTER.

SWORD SWALLOWING

DESPITE VERY REAL DANGERS, SWORD SWALLOWING IS FAR FROM A DYING ART AND A HARDCORE BAND OF ENTHUSIASTS ARE DETERMINED TO KEEP CROWDS THRILLED BY SWALLOWING DOWN A COUPLE OF FEET OF SOLID STEEL FOR THEIR ENTERTAINMENT. BELIEVED TO HAVE ORIGINATED 4,000 YEARS AGO IN INDIA, THE DEADLY FEAT OF SWORD SWALLOWING WAS FEATURED IN THE VERY FIRST RIPLEY'S BELIEVE IT OR NOT! ODDITORIUM IN CHICAGO IN 1933. TODAY THERE ARE NO MORE THAN 100 PROFESSIONAL SWORD SWALLOWERS IN THE WORLD.

Space Cowboy

Chayne "Space Cowboy" Hultgren, a street performer from Australia, is one of the most extreme sword swallowers around. He has swallowed a sword with a 49-lb (22.4-kg) weight suspended from it, and was the first man to swallow a sword underwater—in a tank full of live sharks. Chayne was born with an internal deformation of his digestive system so his stomach sits unusually low. This means that the Space Cowboy can swallow the entire length of a 28½-in (72-cm) sword blade— a blade longer than any other swallower can manage— so that it reaches an inch below his belly button. To conquer the extra long sword, Chayne is able to rearrange his internal organs, elongate his body, and change the shape of his stomach.

In 2008, Chayne Hultgren swallowed 27 swords at once, more than anyone had ever done before.

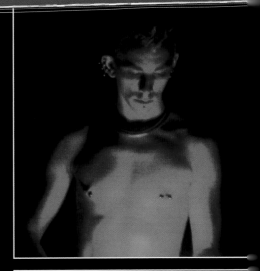

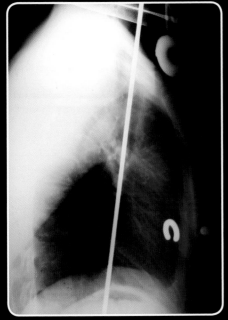

X-ray photographs were taken as Chayne Hultgren swallowed a sword, proving beyond a doubt that there is no illusion involved. He also hammered a 5-in (12.7-cm) nail into his nose at the same time—this is also clearly visible on the X ray.

nail

sword

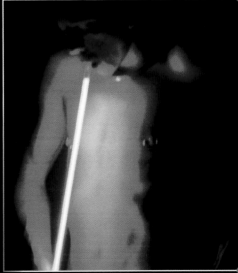

RIPLEY'S ask

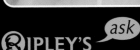

Why did you start sword swallowing? I have been performing street shows since I was eight years old, and as a teenager I began to get tired of the same old traditional circus skills, I wanted to do something more bizarre, more unique, and more extreme. Sword swallowing just seemed like the most adventurous skill that I could learn, but I don't think I quite realized how dangerous my new career choice would be.

Was it hard to learn? Yes, it is very hard to learn. I guess I am lucky that I started to force hoses and other objects down my throat at an early age. You need to learn to control muscles that are usually involuntary and this can take many years. I started training for sword swallowing when I was 16 years old.

In the beginning I swallowed a piece of string with a small piece of food tied to the end. I then moved on to forcing hoses down my throat to train the muscles of my esophagus. Every time a person swallows we have circular muscles that retract in our throat. You need to control these muscles so that when you swallow with a blade down your esophagus these muscles stay open and do not get sliced on the blade.

Doesn't it hurt? No, it doesn't hurt, but it is very uncomfortable. Having a foreign object in your throat instantly makes you gag and vomit, and this is just the first obstacle that you need to overcome in order to swallow a sword. I am constantly pushing myself to make the impossible possible, and in order to do this I need to make the pain I experience obsolete. If you want something enough, pain is no longer an issue.

Have you ever had an accident? I was born with an internal deformation of my digestive system that enables me to swallow a sword deeper than any other sword swallower that has ever lived. When I first started swallowing the long sword I was 20 years old, and in a moment of distraction I sliced my stomach lining in a performance. Backstage I started vomiting blood and was rushed to a hospital. To the doctor's amazement I swallowed an endoscope with no anesthetic! I was prescribed serious drugs to stop any infection. It was a lucky escape. It was ten years before I would attempt this swallow again.

Do you train a lot? On days that I am not performing I do need to keep my internal muscles finely tuned, so I use meditation and internal isolation techniques to stay sword-swallowing fit. In my business any mistake is potentially a deadly one!

What are your future ambitions? I love pushing the boundaries of what people think is possible. I regularly perform what is considered by many to be impossible, in the hope that just by seeing these extreme acts people may consider the endless possibilities of

The "Space Cowboy" swallows the entire length of a 2-ft (60-cm) neon glass tube, which is powered by 2,000 volts and

ohn "Lucky" Ball learned sword swallowing at the age of 12, becoming one of the most
ccomplished sword swallowers of his generation. He is pictured here swallowing a corkscrew
t a Ripley's Odditorium, a feat more dangerous than a straight sword. "Lucky" Ball could
wallow more swords than anyone else at the time, and on one occasion he downed 16.

Ripley's Sword Frights

Sword swallowers have performed at Ripley museums since 1933, when the very first "Odditorium" opened at the Chicago World's Fair. In 1939, Ripley performer Edna Price swallowed electrified neon tubes, and was believed by Robert Ripley to be the first woman to do so, and other entertainers wowed the crowds with their death-defying blade guzzling.

Edna Price, seen here swallowing neon tubes, came from a sword-swallowing family. Her
Aunt Maude died in 1920 after swallowing a sword for the King and Queen of England. Edna
would swallow up to 12 practice swords at the same time, removing the blades one at a time.
She would have her swords chromed each year to protect against nicks and scratches.

ccidents do happen...

vord swallowers often try to swallow objects other than
ords, but this is not always a good idea... In 1891, the sword
allower Patrick Mulraney attempted to swallow a violin bow,
sing him to vomit blood live on stage. He died soon after. In
2, after swallowing a watch and chain and then returning it to
wner, professional sword swallower Fred Lowe swallowed
k, which unfortunately stuck in his throat. It could not be
dged but eventually dropped down into his stomach. It
surgically removed and Lowe made a full recovery. In 1936,
Chicago Daily Tribune reported that experienced sword
ower Bob Roberts died when his trick of swallowing a
un barrel and igniting a fuse literally backfired. In 1947,
Marnio successfully swallowed 2 ft (60 cm) of neon tubing,
lit up inside him for the audience
However, when he attempted
, the glass tube shattered and
rushed to hospital. Francis F.
had been swallowing swords
ears when a 36-in (91-cm) neon
ploded before he could remove
his body in 1969. Surgery was
to remove the glass. Finally,
n sword swallower died
llowing an umbrella in Bonn,
, in 1999. He had accidentally
he button that opened the
while it was still inside him.

Ripley's Sword Swallowing Day

A transatlantic event packed with dangerous stunts took place on February 28, 2009. At precisely 2.28 p.m., 24 sword swallowers swallowed over 100 ft (30 m) of solid steel at Ripley museums from Niagara Falls to London, to mark International Sword Swallowers Awareness Day.

Joseph Grendol swallowed seven swords simultaneously at the Chicago Odditorium in 1934. He could also swallow watches, golf balls, and coins before regurgitating them. Probably his greatest stunt was placing a bayonet on the butt of a rifle, swallowing the bayonet up to the rifle butt, and then shooting the rifle!

Alex Linton

Alex Linton was originally from Ireland. His father was also a sword swallower. At the climax of his act, Linton would throw his final sword into a block of wood on the stage to make sure the audience knew it was real, and sharp!

RIPLEY'S RESEARCH
DO NOT TRY THIS AT HOME!

IT CAN TAKE YEARS TO LEARN HOW TO SWALLOW FULL-SIZED SWORDS (THOSE WHICH ARE AT LEAST 15 IN (38 CM) LONG). PERFORMERS OFTEN START WITH THEIR OWN FINGERS, OR HOUSEHOLD OBJECTS LIKE SPOONS AND KNITTING NEEDLES, TO TRY AND OVERCOME THE GAG REFLEX THAT PREVENTS US FROM SWALLOWING LARGE, DANGEROUS FOREIGN OBJECTS SUCH AS SWORDS!

SWORD SWALLOWING REQUIRES INTENSE CONTROL OF THE BODY, YET PERFORMERS MUST BE FULLY RELAXED AT THE SAME TIME, A PROBLEM WHEN THE MUSCLES INVOLVED USUALLY RESPOND AUTOMATICALLY IN A REFLEX ACTION. PERFORMERS MUST LEARN TO CONTROL ALL THE CIRCULAR MUSCLES IN THE THROAT THAT SQUEEZE FOOD TOWARD YOUR STOMACH. IT IS INCREDIBLY DANGEROUS TO DISTRACT A SWORD SWALLOWER IN THE MIDDLE OF THEIR ACT, AND ANY DISTRACTION COULD PROVE FATAL, AS THE SWORD MUST PASS VERY CLOSE TO CRITICAL AREAS SUCH AS THE WINDPIPE, VITAL BLOOD VESSELS, AND THE HEART. SWALLOWING MULTIPLE SWORDS CAN HAVE A SCISSOR-LIKE EFFECT, GREATLY INCREASING THE DANGER OF CUTS TO THE THROAT.

THE ESOPHAGUS HAS NATURAL CURVES AND KINKS DEPENDING ON THE POSITION OF THE BODY, SO THE SOLID SWORD HAS TO PHYSICALLY STRAIGHTEN THESE OUT AS IT MOVES DOWN. IF THE SWORD IS TOO LONG, OR IF THE PERFORMER LOSES CONTROL, IT CAN DROP INTO THE STOMACH AND CAUSE PERFORATIONS—THIS HAS KILLED MORE THAN ONE SWORD SWALLOWER IN THE PAST.

Balloon Burst!

Jemal Tkeshelashvili from Georgia in the former Soviet Union is able to inflate a hot-water bottle extremely quickly until it bursts, using only his nose. He is so fast that he managed to burst one of the bottles in only 13 seconds at an unusual contest in Tbilisi, Georgia. Jemal also competes as a strongman, and can pull a Boeing Airliner with just his bare hands.

Ⓡ FIVE-DAY SPEECH

At the railway station in Perpignan, France, in January 2009, 62-year-old Catalan local-government worker Lluis Colet spoke for five straight days and four nights—a total of 124 hours—about Spanish painter Salvador Dalí and Catalan culture.

Ⓡ SUPER SHOOTER

Thirty-four-year-old novice Jim Collins of Cambridgeshire, England, beat experienced rivals from as far afield as the United States, Australia, and New Zealand to be crowned world peashooting champion of 2009. The championships, which were started in 1971 by Cambridgeshire school principal John Tyson, who had confiscated a peashooter from a pupil, require competitors to puff peas from a distance of 12 ft (3.6 m) at a 12-in (30-cm) target. Some entrants even use laser-guided peashooters!

Ⓡ GIANT CIGAR

Sixty-five-year-old Cuban Jose Castelar, who has been making cigars since the age of 14, rolled a monster 142-ft-long (43.3-m) cigar in 2009—that's 14 times the height of a school bus.

Ⓡ CHANNEL WINGWALK

In July 2009, Tom Lackey, 89, from West Midlands, England, flew across the English Channel at 1,000 ft (305 m) and more than 100 mph (160 km/h) while strapped to the wings of a vintage airplane. The daredevil grandfather performed his amazing wingwalk over a 22-mi (40-km) stretch of water separating France and England on a plane that was just 20 years younger than him.

Ⓡ JET PACK

Using a jet pack powered by hydrogen peroxide, Eric Scott of Denver, Colorado, clocked a speed of 68 mph (109 km/h) at Knockhill Racing Circuit, Scotland, in May 2009. Although Scott's jet pack currently carries only enough fuel to fly him for 30 seconds, it was sufficient for him to beat a Ford Focus RS car driven by British Touring Car champion Gordon Shedden in a drag race.

Ⓡ IPLEY'S _ask_

What did you eat during your time underwater? For breakfast I ate sausage and cheese. For lunch I had lentil soup, meatballs, chicken, and a banana. For dinner I had more lentil soup, sausage, grilled chicken, and peach. And once a day I had to have sports food.

How did you actually eat your food? The most important thing while you eat something under the water is to make sure that you do not swallow any water. The best way to eat something is to exhale slowly before pushing something in to the mouth. This requires talent and experience.

How did you manage to get any sleep? Between 1 a.m. and 5 a.m. I slept face downward. And during the day I took naps.

What were the conditions like in the tank? The first two days it was really cold. I took my dry suit off and put on my wet suit (I changed underwater) and then it was OK.

Were you able to communicate with the outside world? The hand signals that I improvised allowed me to communicate with my friends. I also had a full-face mask by Ocean Reef Co. that included a communication device.

Ⓡ MUSCLE MAN

At age 80, Abdurakhman Abdulazizov, from the southern Russian republic of Dagestan, can pull a railway carriage by means of a rope tied to his body, and lift an iron girder weighing over 220 lb (100 kg) with his teeth.

Ⓡ SPEEDY JUGGLER

In July 2009, the Czech Republic's Zdenek Bradác, while juggling three balls, made 339 catches in just 60 seconds.

Ⓡ BRIDE PARADE

Sporting full bridal regalia, 110 brides and brides-to-be paraded through Bucharest in June 2009 to promote the institution of marriage in Romania.

Water Home

Cem Karabay, a diver from Turkey, spent five and a half days nonstop living underwater. Surviving on meals put together by an expert nutritionist, and lots of liquids, he managed to eat, sleep, drink, and exercise in his tank measuring 16 x 10 x 10 ft (5 x 3 x 3 m), located outside a shopping mall in Istanbul. His diving teacher, Namik Ekin, had previously lived underwater for 124 hours, but Cem's impressive 135 hours and 2 minutes beat his time. After almost a week underwater, Cem had high blood pressure and an eye infection, but he emerged with a greater desire to go back—the next time for ten days!

Ⓡ PRESSING ENGAGEMENT

On January 10, 2009, 86 scuba divers dived 173 ft (52.7 m) to the bottom of a flooded quarry in Monmouthshire, Wales, and ironed clothes on ironing boards at the same time.

Ⓡ BED JUMP

Over a period of 16 hours in May 2009, around 20,000 people in four cities—New York, London, Paris, and Shanghai—jumped on four giant beds. The beds, which took a team of 100 people five weeks to build and incorporated over 200,000 nuts and bolts and six tons of steel, measured 49 x 33 ft (15 x 10 m) and were each topped with 30 double mattresses and a huge super-sized duvet that could cover 65 regular double beds.

Jyothi Raj believes he was given the gift of climbing and is happy to teach his skills to anyone who wants to learn, provided they use harnesses.

Real Life
SPIDERMAN

JYOTHI RAJ HAS INCREDIBLE CLIMBING ABILITIES WHEREBY HE IS SEEMINGLY ABLE TO GLUE HIMSELF TO WALLS WITHOUT ANY HARNESSES OR ASSISTANCE, AND EVEN MANAGES TO HANG UPSIDE DOWN USING ONLY HIS FEET! JYOTHI, A CONSTRUCTION WORKER FROM KARNATAKA, INDIA, SPENDS HIS DAYS CLIMBING UP AND DOWN BUILDING SITES, USUALLY ON BAMBOO SCAFFOLDING, WHICH CAN BE VERY DANGEROUS. HE STARTED PRACTICING FREE CLIMBING EVERY DAY UNTIL HE WAS ABLE TO CLING TO THE WALLS, USING JUST HIS HANDS, AT 90-DEGREE ANGLES AND EVEN UPSIDE DOWN. HE STATES HE HAS NEVER USED SAFETY EQUIPMENT TO CLIMB AND ISN'T AFRAID OF FALLING. EVERY SUNDAY, JYOTHI COMES TO THE FAMOUS FORT AT CHITRADURGA TO ENTERTAIN HIS FANS. REACHING HEIGHTS OF UP TO 300 FT (90 M), JYOTHI HAS SCALED EVERY WALL POSSIBLE AT THE FORT AND IS READY TO MOVE ON TO BIGGER BUILDINGS AND MOUNTAINS. CLAIMING HE HASN'T HAD AN ACCIDENT IN FOUR YEARS, HIS ULTIMATE GOAL IS TO BE LIKE ALAIN ROBERT, THE FAMOUS FRENCH FREE CLIMBER KNOWN AS THE "HUMAN SPIDER," WHO HAS CLIMBED MANY OF THE WORLD'S TALLEST STRUCTURES, SOME OF THEM OVER 650 FT (200 M) HIGH.

BED ROCK

A 1980s' INVENTION ALLOWS MOUNTAIN CLIMBERS WITH PARTICULARLY STRONG NERVES TO SLEEP THOUSANDS OF FEET UP VERTICAL CLIFF FACES. THE PORTALEDGE IS A SMALL PORTABLE TENT, SUSPENDED BY ONLY ROPES AND FABRIC ATTACHED TO TEMPORARY ANCHOR POINTS JAMMED IN ROCK CRACKS. THE TENTS LOOK PERILOUS BUT ARE REPORTED TO BE SURPRISINGLY STABLE; SOME CLIMBERS EVEN TAKE THE RISK OF LIGHTING GAS STOVES INSIDE TO COOK FOOD AND MELT SNOW. IT IS RECOMMENDED THAT PORTALEDGE OCCUPANTS REMAIN HARNESSED TO THE CLIFF FACE WHEN ASLEEP, IN CASE THEY HAVE A HABIT OF FALLING OUT OF BED.

Don't Look Down

This picture is the right way up! In the skies over Illinois in 2009, a fearless group of 108 daredevils jumped from a plane at 18,000 ft (5,486 m), reaching speeds of 180 mph (290 km/h) as they plummeted head first toward the ground in tight formation. After 40 seconds of individual free fall, the jumpers made the risky mid-flight maneuvers required to get themselves into position, and held on tight, completing the formation only a few seconds before breaking apart for landing.

℞ BUSY DAY

On August 4, 1982, Texan-born outfielder Joel Youngblood got hits for two different Major League baseball teams in two different cities on the same day. In the afternoon he played for the New York Mets at Wrigley Field, Chicago, Illinois, against the Chicago Cubs. Then, after he had been traded, he appeared in a night game for the Montreal Expos in Philadelphia, Pennsylvania.

℞ STILETTO SPRINT

At a race in Nanning, Guangxi Province, China, all the runners wear high heels—both men and women! Male runners must wear shoes with heels at least 3 in (8 cm) high, while women have to run in 4-in (10-cm) stilettos because they are more used to wearing high heels.

℞ HOOP HOPPER

Thirteen-year-old Anna Schmeissing of Chicago, Illinois, can play basketball while hopping on a pogo stick.

℞ GOLF MARATHON

Tom Bucci of Latham, New York, played 1,801 holes of golf in a week at the Albany Country Club in June 2009. Despite losing 75 minutes to a thunderstorm, Bucci played 15 rounds (270 holes) every day, averaging 90 strokes per round, including 32 birdies and his first-ever hole-in-one.

℞ CALORIE BURN

A cyclist competing in the Tour de France can burn up to 10,000 calories during a mountain-stage day—that's more than four times as much as someone walking for 75 minutes a day for an entire week.

℞ SNOW GOLF

An Italian ski resort stages a golf tournament in up to 3 ft (90 cm) of snow and at an altitude of 5,250 ft (1600 m). Players use brightly colored orange balls on the specially built nine-hole course at the Rein resort in Taufers.

℞ GREAT NATE

Nate Kmic of the Mount Union, Ohio, college football team is the only U.S. college football player to run more than 8,000 rushing yards, which he did during his college career between 2005 and 2008.

℞ HANDICAP GOLFER

Forty-five-year-old former soldier Alan Perrin, who is almost blind and has only one arm, hit a hole-in-one at his local Exminster Golf Club, near Exeter, Devon, England, in April 2009. He and his golfing partner could hardly believe it when, after several minutes of searching, they finally found the yellow ball in the hole.

℞ REAL GLOBETROTTER

Marques Haynes of the Harlem Globetrotters played basketball for more than 50 years, making his final appearance in 1997 when he was in his early seventies! He played more than 12,000 games in 97 countries, traveling more than four million miles (that's about 160 times around the world). He learned his famously fantastic dribbling skills from his sisters and could dribble the ball six times a second, his hand just a few inches above the floor.

℞ DOWNHILL SKIER

Austrian Alpine skier Balthasar Egger traveled approximately 232 mi (374 km) downhill on skis in 24 hours at Heiligenblut, Austria, in March 2009.

℞ GOAL RUSH

During a 2008 Olympic pre-qualifying tournament, the Slovakian women's ice-hockey team defeated Bulgaria 82 goals to 0, scoring at the rate of more than one goal a minute.

Living the High Life

HEINZ ZAK IS NOT YOUR ORDINARY THRILL-SEEKER OR ADRENALINE JUNKIE. ALTHOUGH HE RISKS HIS LIFE ON A REGULAR BASIS HUNDREDS OF FEET UP IN THE AIR, HEINZ SAYS THAT HE PERFORMS SUCH PERILOUS FEATS TO ACHIEVE A STATE OF INNER PEACE AND TRANQUILITY. "HIGHLINING" IS AN EXTREME FORM OF "SLACKLINING," WHICH INVOLVES A STRIP OF NYLON 1 IN (2.5 CM) THICK STRUNG RELATIVELY LOOSELY HIGH ABOVE WILD TERRAIN OR WATER. THIS MEANS THAT THE LINE FLEXES AND EVEN BOUNCES, MAKING THE SPORT DIFFERENT FROM TRADITIONAL TIGHTROPE WALKING. INTENSE FOCUS ALLOWS HEINZ TO WALK CALMLY ACROSS THE LINE. SINCE THE 1980S, HE HAS TRAVELED THE WORLD SEARCHING FOR THE PERFECT PLACE TO PRACTICE HIS DEATH-DEFYING FEATS.

Bride to Bee

When Li Wenhua and Yan Hongxia, workers at Nanhu forestry commission in Ning'an, China, decided to tie the knot, they made sure they invited some of their coworkers—in the form of tens of thousands of honeybees. A carefully placed queen bee attracted the entire swarm, forming living-insect material for an alternative pair of wedding outfits. The number of people stung at the wedding is unknown.

ℝ ARCTIC MARATHON

Wearing only shorts and a pair of sandals, Dutchman Wim Hof completed a 2009 marathon in sub-zero temperatures 200 mi (322 km) north of the Arctic Circle. His body was exposed to temperatures of –13°F (–25°C) as he finished the 26-mi (42-km) trek in 5 hours 25 minutes.

ℝ AROUND BRITAIN

Starting and finishing in London, English comedian Eddie Izzard ran 1,105 mi (1,778 km) around Britain from July 26 to September 15, 2009—the equivalent of running 43 marathons in 51 days.

ℝ WORM CHARMERS

Ten-year-old Sophie Smith of Cheshire, England, coaxed 567 worms up from the ground in 30 minutes to win Britain's 2009 World Worm Charming Championships. Techniques used to encourage worms to the surface included a man playing the xylophone with bottles and a woman who tap-danced to the theme from *Star Wars*.

ℝ MICHIGAN SWIM

By completing a 26-hour, 34-mi (55-km) swim across Lake Michigan in 2009, Paula Stephanson of Belleville, Ontario, Canada, became only the second person to swim across all five Great Lakes. Her first Great Lake swim was across Lake Ontario in 1996 at age 17.

ℝ IRON MAN

Japanese athlete Keizo Yamada, known as the "Iron Man," ran three marathons in 2009—at 81 years of age. He completed the Tokyo marathon in 5 hours 34 minutes 50 seconds and kept fit by jogging 12 mi (20 km) every day.

ℝ BRIDGE FLIP

Australian motorcycle stunt rider Robbie Maddison performed a no-handed backflip while jumping the 25-ft (7.6-m) gap between the raised spans of London's Tower Bridge in July 2009. He raced up one side of the raised bridge, flew through the air 100 ft (30 m) above the water and made the backflip before landing on the south side of the bridge.

ℝ BASKETBALL SPIN

Cheshire Jets basketball team from Chester, England, gathered more than 100 people to spin basketballs on their fingers simultaneously in July 2009.

ℝ ELVIS WARDROBE

Vince Everett of London, England, owned more than 3,000 items of Elvis Presley memorabilia, including 14 of Elvis' jackets.

ℝ STRAIT CROSSING

Ben Morrison-Jack and James Weight kite-surfed across the Bass Strait in September 2009 from Tasmania to mainland Australia—a distance of 155 mi (250 km).

ℝ ROPE TRICK

Damian Cooksey of East Bay, California, landed a frontflip on a 1-in-thick (2.5-cm) slackline—a rope that is not taut. In 2007, in Munich, Germany, he walked 506 ft (154 m) on a slackline without falling off.

ℝ FEMALE FORMATION

Jumping from nine planes at an altitude of 17,000 ft (5,180 m), 181 female skydivers from 31 countries joined together in formation above Perris, California, in September 2009.

ℝ PIE FIGHT

More than 250 people turned up to take part in a mass custard-pie fight at Colchester, Essex, England, in 2009. Around 650 pies—filled with 53 gal (200 l) of custard—were thrown during the battle.

ℝ GROUP SHOWER

One hundred and fifty strangers in swimsuits showered together in a specially constructed 40,000-sq-ft (3,716-sq-m) structure at Gurnee, Illinois, in 2009. The huge shower, designed to hold around 600 people elbow to elbow, had 40 shower nozzles and took 7½ hours to build.

Heat Seeker

As unusual hobbies go, it's a dangerous choice. Keith Malcolm from Aberdeen, Scotland, dresses in several layers of flame-retardant clothing before he's doused in gasoline and set alight like a human torch. He then runs as far as he can before the flames overwhelm him and firefighters put him out. In 2009, Malcolm sped 259 ft (79 m) in aid of charity.

Chad was able to keep two 300-horsepower airplanes grounded on a runway with only his arms for just over one minute.

MAN OF STRENGTH

CHAD CAN RIP LICENSE PLATES IN TWO...

WISCONSIN
A 517 394
OCT   TRUCK   06

Chad suffered no ill effects after being pinned to a bed of 12-in (30-cm) nails by 848 lb (385 kg) of concrete until each block was smashed with a sledgehammer on Sixth Avenue, New York.

...AND A PACK OF CARDS!

RIPLEY'S ask

What made you begin breaking ice?

I've been training in the martial arts my entire life. My mom went into labor in one of my dad's martial arts schools and there it began. With years of mental and physical training and conditioning, I have been able to do amazing breaks and feats of strength.

How much training do you do?

What stunt I'm attempting next will determine how I train, but on average I run 2 miles a day and work out for about four or five days a week.

How do you break 16 blocks of ice in one strike?

There is a lot of setup and preparation required when attempting an ice break this large. Unlike concrete, ice starts to sweat and can slide side to side when you hit it. Everything has to be perfect, including the strike, to make a successful break.

Does it hurt?

When I am attempting a record ice break I know it's going to hurt, but I also know there is always enough crushed ice laying around afterward if I need to ice down my wrist.

How do you keep from getting injured?

I have not sustained any major injuries from any stunt I have attempted to date. There is a lot of conditioning, setup, and preparation that goes into what I do and that helps minimize the risk.

Do you have any tips for aspiring strength athletes?

My advice to aspiring athletes, or anyone who wants to do something out of the ordinary, is this. "Most people never reach their goals in life because they are afraid of failing and they allow fear to rob them of the potential that they had to be successful. Anything is possible! Live without fear. Live without limits."

What are your plans for feats of strength in the future?

I am currently training for one of my most extreme stunts yet. I'm going to attempt to hold back a Lamborghini by hand at full throttle for 8 seconds.

ICE BREAKER

CHAD NETHERLAND IS A BLACK-BELT MARTIAL ARTIST WHO SPECIALIZES IN BREAKING HARD OBJECTS WITH HIS BARE HANDS. IN 2009, IN ONE STRIKE, CHAD DESTROYED SIXTEEN 75-LB (34-KG) BLOCKS OF ICE THAT WERE 6 IN (15 CM) THICK, BREAKING A TOTAL OF 1,200 LB (544 KG) OF ICE—ENOUGH FOR A GROUP OF ADULTS TO STAND ON. CHAD, FROM MYRTLE BEACH, SOUTH CAROLINA, LEARNED EVERYTHING HE DOES FROM HIS FATHER, WHO WAS ALSO A WORLD-CLASS MARTIAL-ARTS EXPERT. HE HAS SMASHED 50 BLOCKS OF ICE IN 19 SECONDS LIVE ON TELEVISION AND STOPPED TWO LIGHT AIRCRAFT FROM TAKING OFF FOR OVER A MINUTE WITH ONLY HIS ARMS. IN 2003, HE LAID ON A BED OF 12-IN (30-CM) NAILS WHILE CONCRETE BLOCKS WEIGHING 848 LB (385 KG) WERE SMASHED WITH A SLEDGEHAMMER ON HIS CHEST!

ACKNOWLEDGMENTS

COVER (t) www.JW-SPORTFOTO.de, (b) www.lloydimages.com, BACK COVER wetsuits bydiddo.com ©; 4 Chad Netherland; 6–7 PPL Media;
8 (t) Shaun Curry/AFP/Getty Images, (b) Reuters/Chaiwat Subprasom; 9 Dave Thompson/PA Wire/Press Association Images; 10 Andrew J.K. Tan;
11 (sp) Walt Seng /Getty Images; 12 (b/l) National Museum of the United States Air Force, (t/r, b/r) wetsuits bydiddo.com ©; 13 Mery Nunez/
Barcroft Media Ltd.; 14–15 Michael Martin/Barcroft Media Ltd.; 16–17 Marcus Brandt/DPA/Press Association Images; 18 www.lloydimages.com
19 www.JW-SPORTFOTO.de; 20 Niall Carson/PA Archive/Press Association Images; 21 The Space Cowboy; 24 AFP/Getty Images; 25 Wenn.com;
26–27 Niklas Halle'n/Barcroft Media Ltd.; 28 (sp) Topher Donahue/Getty Images, (t/l) Photolibrary.com; 29 Norman Kent/Barcroft Media Ltd.;
30 (sp) Barcroft Media, (b) © EuroPics[CEN]; 31 M & Y Agency Ltd/Rex Features; 32–33 Chad Netherland

Key: t = top, b = bottom, c = center, l = left, r = right, sp = single page, dp = double page

All other photos are from Ripley Entertainment Inc.
Every attempt has been made to acknowledge correctly and contact copyright holders and we apologize in advance
for any unintentional errors or omissions, which will be corrected in future editions.